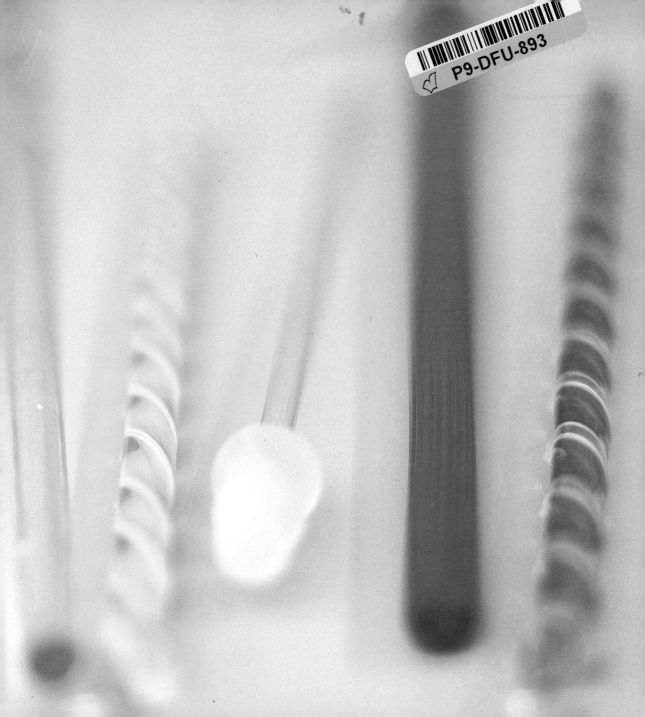

coolers
and summer
cocktails

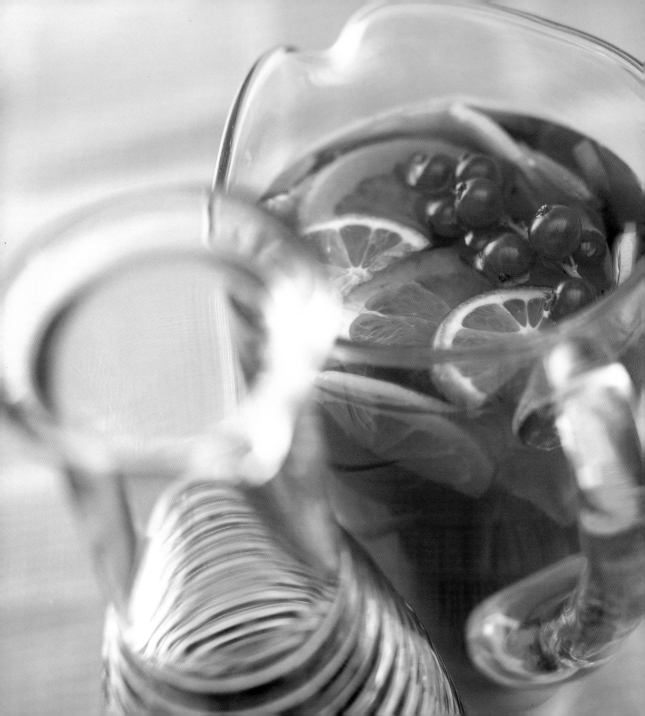

coolers
and summer
cocktails

elsa petersen-schepelern

photography by

james merrell

RYLAND
PETERS
& SMALL

LONDON NEW YORK

Art Editor **Penny Stock**

Assistant Designer **Lucy Hamilton**

Editor **Elsa Petersen-Schepelern**

Creative Director **Jacqui Small**

Publishing Director **Anne Ryland**

Production **Kate Mackillop**

Food Stylist **David Peacock**

Stylist **Wei Tang**

Author Photograph **Francis Loney**

My thanks to my sister Kirsten, Nowelle Valentino-Capezza, Peter Bray, and Sheridan Lear for their enthusiastic help and advice, and to Lucy Hamilton for her presentation design. Thanks also to Tim and the summer gathering at Le Mandorle in Tuscany for their critical assessment of Morocco Mary.

First published in the United States in 1998
This edition published 2003
by Ryland Peters & Small, Inc.
519 Broadway, 5th Floor
New York, NY 10012
www.rylandpeters.com

10 9 8 7 6 5 4

Printed and bound in China

ISBN 978 1 84172 430 0

Library of Congress Cataloging-in-Publication data is available on request.

coolers
and summer
cocktails

Drinks in the garden, lunch on the deck, barbecues, tennis parties, and sunbathing— all essential summer pastimes requiring the drinks in this book. You'll find recipes for children and adults, drinks with and without alcohol, cocktails for one, or for casts of thousands (or quite a few, anyway!)

Old-fashioned lemonade and ginger beer are great for hot summer days, while cocktails like Mint Mojito and Negroni should definitely wait until the sun is over the yardarm! But you can always make them less intoxicating by adding a mixer and serving them in a tall glass.

The book includes many recipes you won't find in other books—try, for instance, a Morocco Mary (a traditional Bloody Mary, but made with harissa paste, the gorgeous Moroccan spiced chili purée).

Most ingredients used in the book are widely available in shops selling wine and spirits, as well as in gourmet stores and many of the larger supermarkets.

Moroccan mint tea is served hot in tiny engraved and gilded glasses—it's the perfect finish to a spicy Moroccan meal and helps oil the wheels of conversation in countless tea shops across the country. I like it just as much chilled and poured over ice as a cool summer drink. I prefer to make it in a French press coffee pot, so you don't have to bother with straining or fishing out the leaves. If you don't have a French press, you can make it in a teapot or a big pitcher, then strain into another pitcher before chilling and serving.

moroccan iced mint tea

1 large bunch of fresh mint sprigs

mint sprigs, to serve

sugar, to taste, served separately

Fill a French press coffee pot with mint, add boiling water, and let cool. Push the plunger, then pour the tea into a pitcher. Chill, then serve in Moroccan tea glasses with mint and a separate bowl of sugar.

Serves 4–6

summer coolers

fresh homemade
ginger beer

This ginger beer is quicker than the traditional kind (which fills your cellar with bottles that explode over the following weeks). I also think the taste is fresher and brighter. Don't peel the ginger if you chop it in a food processor—just cut it up coarsely then pulse until well minced. The skin will give the beer extra flavor.

4 oz. fresh ginger, grated or chopped

zest and juice of 2 limes

2 cloves

1 cup sugar (brown gives better color)

soda or sparkling mineral water, to serve

Put all ingredients in a large French press coffee pot or pitcher, add 4 cups boiling water, then stir until the sugar dissolves. Cool, plunge or strain, then chill well. To serve, half-fill glasses with the mixture and top with soda or sparkling mineral water.

Serves 4

apple
lemonade

This recipe is best made with tart-tasting cooking apples—they turn to delicious apple-flavored foam when boiled. For a much quicker result, use fresh apple juice, omit the sugar, add the fresh lemon juice, and fill with mineral water.

2–3 apples, preferably cooking apples, unpeeled, chopped into small pieces

sugar, to taste

ice

juice of 1 lemon

sparkling mineral water, to serve

Put the apples in a saucepan, cover with cold water, bring to a boil, and simmer until soft. Sieve, pressing the pulp through the sieve with a spoon. Add sugar to taste, stir until dissolved, then let cool.

To serve, pack a pitcher with ice, half-fill with the apple juice, add the lemon juice, and top with mineral water. Alternatively, serve in individual glasses.

Serves 4

a quick and **easy apple** drink

for children or grownups

jamaican iced ginger
sorrel tea

Jamaican sorrel is the flower of a native hibiscus, sold fresh or dried in Caribbean stores or in health food shops, where it is known as "red hibiscus tea." It's also known as "rosella" in Australia and New Zealand, and is used to make jam. It's an unusual, sophisticated taste, and if you like vaguely bitter flavors, you'll love it!

1 tablespoon ginger purée
¼ cup dried sorrel flowers
or hibiscus tea
¼ cup sugar
ice
a twist of lime

Put the first 3 ingredients in a French press coffee pot. Add boiling water. Plunge when liquid is light purple, then cool and chill. Serve over ice with a twist of lime. To serve as a weaker drink, top up with gingerale, soda, or mineral water. The cocktail below usually has lots of sugar, but I prefer it less sweet.
Serves 4–8

Variation:
Sorrel Rum Cocktail
Put ¼ cup dried sorrel, a curl of orange zest, 1 cinnamon stick, 6 cloves, and 1–2 cups sugar, in a French press coffee pot. Add 6 cups boiling water, stir well, then push the plunger. Add 2 extra cloves and a cinnamon stick to the top, cool, and chill. To serve, pour over ice, then add 3 tablespoons rum and a cinnamon stick for swizzling.
Serves 6–8

pineapple
strawberryade

A summer cooler that's simply the most glorious color and tastes like heaven!

zest and strained juice of 2 lemons

strained juice of 2 oranges

1 medium pineapple, peeled and cored

2 tablespoons confectioners' sugar

ice

10–12 ripe red strawberries

sliced strawberries or a curl of citrus peel, to serve

Put the pineapple, strawberries, lemon zest and confectioners' sugar in a blender with about ½ cup ice water. Purée until smooth. Add the orange and lemon juices and another ½ cup ice water. Taste and add extra sugar if necessary (depending on the sweetness of the fruit). Pour into a pitcher of ice and top with sliced berries and a twist of orange or lemon peel.

Serves 6–8

a gingery Caribbean variation on one
of the great **Indian classics**

mango
ginger lassi

This mango lassi is made with the Indian Alphonso—the world's greatest mango. If you can't find one fresh, purée any variety of sweet mango in a blender. The good-quality canned Alphonso mango purée sold by Asian grocers can also be used instead (and tastes spectacular).

1 cup Alphonso mango purée
1 cup plain low-fat yogurt
1 tablespoon ginger purée
crushed ice
4 cups Jamaican ginger beer

Put the first 4 ingredients in a pitcher and mix well (I used a pair of chopsticks). Top up with ginger beer and serve.
Serves 6–8 or more

cranberry
cooler

Cranberry mixed with citrus juice is a marriage made in heaven—the prettiest cloudy pink. Try the virgin version below, or the stronger variation (right). To make the Carrot Cooler, use freshly-crushed carrot juice, which you can now buy in sandwich bars, supermarkets, and health food shops. Just make sure you buy the fresh kind—the canned or bottled kind isn't suitable.

crushed ice

1 cup cranberry juice

1 cup orange juice

sparkling mineral water

a twist of orange peel, to serve

Fill a pitcher with crushed ice, add the cranberry and orange juices, and stir well. Top up with sparkling mineral water and serve with a twist of orange peel.

Serves 1–2

Sea Breeze

Use grapefruit juice instead of orange, omit the mineral water, and add ½ cup vodka.

Serves 2–3

Lime and Carrot Juice Cooler

Put 1 cup carrot juice in a cocktail shaker with the juice of 1 lime, 1 tablespoon ginger purée or juice from preserved ginger, then fill with crushed ice. Shake, then strain into tall glasses packed with ice and serve with shreds of lemon zest.

A shot of gin or vodka turns this drink a real pick-me-up!

Serves 1

rhubarb berryade

Make this unusual, old-fashioned drink with pretty red rhubarb for an utterly stunning color, or add a dash of Grenadine to exaggerate the effect.

1 lb. rhubarb, trimmed and sliced

2 tablespoons sugar

6 strawberries

rind and juice of 1 lemon

ice

sparkling mineral water, to taste

Put the rhubarb in a saucepan, then add the sugar and at least 4 cups boiling water. Stew until the rhubarb is very soft. Add the strawberries and boil hard for 1 minute, then strain into a pitcher and cool. To serve, pour into a pitcher of ice, stir in the lemon juice, and top with mineral water.

Serves 4–8

Variation:

Orange and Rhubarb Tea

Another great drink to make with rhubarb! Stew 1 lb. rhubarb in a saucepan with ½ cup sugar, 4 cups boiling water, and the rind of a lemon. Strain, discarding the solids. Cool, chill, add 2 cups iced tea, the juice of 1 lemon and 1 orange, and stir. Add 1 thinly sliced orange and serve with extra sugar, so everyone can sweeten to taste.

Serves 4–6

We've all had commercial lemonade, which is little more than fizzy sugar water. Real lemonade, on the other hand, is cool and refreshing and actually tastes of lemons. This recipe is for good old-fashioned lemonade, taken from hand-written recipe books lent by aunts and grandmothers. It always reminds me of tennis parties, wicker chairs on the lawn, drinks in the cool shade of the veranda, and lemonade served by my mother, the last woman in the world to own a parasol!

real lemonade

3–4 tablespoons sugar

a pinch of salt

1½ tablespoons lemon juice

ice cubes

mint leaves

a few slices of lemon

Put the sugar and salt in a saucepan with 4 cups boiling water and boil for 2 minutes. Chill and add the lemon juice, then serve in a frosted glass pitcher with ice, mint, and a few thin lemon slices floating on top.

Serves 2–4

citrus coolers

a delicious, old-fashioned drink,
great for **summer parties**

old-fashioned
orangeade

2 oranges, sliced and seeded, but

unpeeled, plus a curl of orange peel

1 lemon, sliced and seeded,

but unpeeled

ice

¼ cup sugar, or to taste

Put the sliced oranges, lemon, and sugar in a large pitcher, add 4–6 cups boiling water, cover, cool, and chill. Serve strained over glasses of ice with a curl of orange peel. Alternatively, double the quantity of fruit. Peel the rinds, discarding any white pith. Put the rinds in a large pitcher, sprinkle with 2 tablespoons sugar, then squeeze the citrus juices and add to the pitcher. Fill with boiling water and let stand until cool. Taste and stir in extra sugar if necessary. Strain into a pitcher of ice and serve in tall glasses over ice.

Serves 2–4

These old-fashioned drinks are not fizzy like modern soft drinks. For fizz, make a stronger mixture by decreasing the water quantity, then serve in glasses topped up with sparkling mineral water or soda.

Variation:

Granny's Orangeade

This variation is very similar, but tastes a little more "orangy." Peel the rinds of 4 oranges, leaving the white pith behind. Put the rinds into a pitcher with ¼ cup sugar, then add the juice of the oranges and 1 lemon. Add 4 cups boiling water, let stand until cool, strain, and serve over ice. You can also use less water and add soda or mineral water when serving.

Serves 2–4

These soothing, cooling, old-fashioned drinks are incredibly easy to make since the invention of the French press coffee pot with the plunger. In Victorian times, platoons of kitchenmaids would boil up the lemon and barley, strain it through cheesecloth into enormous pitchers, let it cool, then try to chill it with whatever technology was available in the Big House at the time. Lucky us—we have refrigerators and ice. So much easier! The Apple Water variation is wonderful.

Variation:

Apple Water

Purée the juice and zest of ½ lemon, 3 cored, sliced apples, and 1 tablespoon sugar in a food processor. Transfer to a French press coffee pot and add 3 cups water. Cool, plunge, chill, and serve.

lemon
barley water

2 tablespoons pearl barley

grated zest and juice of 1 large, unwaxed lemon

2 teaspoons sugar

crushed ice

a curl of lemon peel

Put the barley in a pan, cover with 6 cups boiling water, and simmer for 30 minutes. Strain into a French press coffee pot, then stir in the sugar, lemon zest, and lemon juice. Cool, plunge, chill, then serve over crushed ice with a curl of lemon peel.

Serves 2–4

indian fresh
lime soda

I have been to India many times, and it never seems to get any cooler! My favourite thirst-quencher—served everywhere from five-star hotels to village truck-stops—is this fresh lime soda, served either with salt or sugar (or, in my case, plain). You wouldn't think that salty drinks could be at all pleasant, but Indians serve fresh lime sodas and yogurt lassi drinks with a pinch of salt, and they are incredibly cooling. Try it and see!

Surprisingly, the French variation, the Citron Pressé, is very similar. Lemon juice is squeezed into a glass, and served with a separate pitcher of ice water and a bowl of sugar. I think this is just the perfect cooler in the middle of a hard day's shopping in Paris!

1–2 limes

1 small bottle soda water

sugar or sea salt, to taste

crushed ice or ice cubes (optional)

Squeeze the juice from the limes into a tall glass. Serve with a bottle of soda or sparkling mineral water, and small dishes of salt or sugar, according to taste. Crushed ice or ice cubes may also be added.

Serves 1

Variation:

Citron Pressé

Squeeze the juice of 1 lemon into a tall glass. Serve with a pitcher of ice water, a small dish of sugar, and a long spoon.

Serves 1

pimms

This traditional English summertime drink is perfect for tennis parties and polo matches. When borage is in flower, freeze the pretty blue blossoms in ice cubes for out-of-season drinks. Allow 1 cup per drink, and at least 2 drinks per person if serving Pimms for a party (be prepared for repeat orders!) But take care—this delicious cooler is very strong.

1 part Pimms*
3 parts gingerale, lemonade, or soda
borage flowers
curls of cucumber peel
sliced lemons and sprigs of mint
ice

Put all ingredients into a jug of ice and serve.
Serves 1 or a party

*Pimms is available in specialist liquor stores.

party drinks

mint mojito

The Caribbean and Central America have created some fabulous taste combinations, often based on rum. A Mojito is essentially a rum julep, and you can make it in the same way as the julep on page 52. However, being lazy, I like mine made in a blender, and just love the amazing color produced by the blended mint leaves. Traditional recipes use soda water as a top-up, but I prefer sparkling mineral water. This is also great without the rum, but either way, it's a perfect summer cooler!

½ cup white rum
juice of 1 large lime
¼ cup sugar, or to taste
a large handful of fresh mint sprigs
ice cubes
soda water or sparkling mineral water
mint sprigs, to serve
a curl of lime zest

Put the rum, lime juice, sugar, 4 ice cubes, ½ cup mineral water, and mint leaves in a blender, then purée. Strain into a pitcher, then pour into tall glasses packed with ice. Top with soda or mineral water to taste, add lime zest and a sprig of mint, and serve. To serve a larger number of people, increase the quantities accordingly, and instead of pouring into glasses, pour into a pitcher one-third full of ice, then top with sparkling mineral water and serve.
Serves 1–4

tropical
sangria

Spanish Sangria with a South American twist! Use any fruit, but include tropicals, like mango, pineapple, or starfruit. Don't use any that go "furry," such as melon or strawberries. This is great for a summer party in the garden, and you can produce a non-alcoholic kind for children and non-drinkers using gingerale or lemonade instead of the champagne.

1 ripe mango, finely sliced
1 lime, finely sliced
1 lemon, finely sliced
½ pineapple, wedged and finely sliced
3 kiwifruit, sliced
1 starfruit (carambola), sliced
3 tablespoons sugar
1 bottle chilled champagne

Slice the fruit into a punch bowl. Sprinkle with sugar and set aside for 30 minutes. Top with champagne just before serving.
Serves 4–8

Variations:
Quick Neapolitan Sangria
Half-fill a punch bowl with ice, add 1 bottle orange squash and 2 bottles light red wine.
Serves 8–12

Neapolitan Red Peach Sangria
Half-fill a punch bowl with ice, add 1 bottle light red wine, 1 cup peach nectar, mint sprigs, and 1 sliced peach.
Serves 4

This punch—great for a party—is very
strong, so if you want to give people more
than one glass, make it gentler by adding
a bottle or two of ginger beer, gingerale,
or sparkling mineral water. If you can't
find ginger wine, use dry sherry mixed
with 2 tablespoons ginger purée.

6 limes (3 juiced, 3 sliced)
½ bottle ginger wine
1 bottle (750 ml) vodka or white rum
sugar, to taste
3 lemons, sliced
1 starfruit (carambola), sliced
1 pineapple, cut lengthwise into long
wedges, then crosswise into triangles
sprigs of mint, to serve

mighty **jamaican**
punch

Mix the lime juice, ginger wine, and vodka
or rum with the sugar until dissolved.
Fill a punch bowl with ice, add the sliced
fruit, and pour over the ginger wine mixture.
Stir well and serve with sprigs of mint.
Serves about 16–20

caribbean **tea** punch

Make this punch with a flavored tea like Lapsang Souchong or Earl Grey. I make mine in a small French press coffee pot so I can press the plunger as soon as the tea reaches the right color—30 seconds to 1 minute, before the tannin is released. The scent of lemon mixes beautifully with the rich scent of rum. For parties, make a big pot of tea, mix with half its volume of rum, sweeten, and serve with mixers.

1 cup weak black tea

1 tablespoon sugar

crushed ice

½ cup dark rum or golden rum

peeled zest of ½ lemon

1 lemon slice (optional)

Stir the sugar into the hot tea. Let cool, then stir well. Fill a glass with ice, add the tea, stir in the rum and lemon zest, and serve with a slice of lemon.

Serves 1–2

Variations:

Mango Rum Punch

Mix 1 cup mango purée, 1 teaspoon lemon juice, a pinch of cardamom, and 2 cups golden rum. Stir well, pour over ice, and serve, topped with a few cardamom seeds. (For the best flavor, crush 6 green cardamom pods, extract the black seeds, and discard the green pods.)

Serves 3–6

Planter's Punch

There must be hundreds of combinations for Planter's Punch, and their composition probably depended on where the planter lived—this one comes from sugar-growing areas such as Australia and the Caribbean. In a large pitcher, put 1 cup white rum, 1 cup pineapple juice (freshly crushed if possible), 1 cup mango purée or mango juice, the grated zest and juice of 1 large lime, and a dash of Angostura Bitters. Stir and serve over ice, with a cinnamon swizzle stick.

Serves 3–6

the Caribbean is the source of some of **the greatest** rum cocktails

kumquat ratafia

Ratafias are simple to make—just fruits macerated in brandy. Serve as a small drink or topped up with mineral water.

kumquats (see method)
sugar (see method)
1 cinnamon stick
3 cloves
brandy (see method)

Fill a large preserving jar with kumquats that have been washed and pricked several times with a skewer or needle. Fill the container one-third full with sugar, add the cinnamon and cloves, top up with brandy, and set aside for about 2 months. Serve the liquid as a liqueur, poured over crushed ice as a cocktail, or as a long drink with a mixer, such as mineral water, soda, or lemonade. The fruit is wonderful sliced and served in fruit desserts, or pan-fried in butter and served with meat or game.
Makes 1 jar, about 4 cups

Variation:

Spiced Orange Ratafia
Grate the zest of 6 big oranges and squeeze the juice into an 8-cup preserving jar. Add 2 cups sugar, ½ teaspoon ground coriander, and 1 cinnamon stick. Stir until the sugar dissolves and let stand for 30–60 minutes. Add 5 cups brandy, cover with a lid, and shake the jar. Set aside for 2 months, shaking the jar from time to time. Use as in the main recipe.

Thailand meets the South of France—with some **variations** from Southern Italy

mango kir

Thailand meets the South of France—or Southern Italy in the variations to the right! For the Mango Kir, use canned mango purée (preferably made from Indian Alphonso mangoes), or purée a fresh ripe mango in a blender with a little ice water and 1 tablespoon of lemon juice to help the mango keep its color. For a non-alcoholic version, replace the champagne with gingerale.

2 cups mango purée

2–4 tablespoons ginger purée

(optional)

1 cup crushed ice

ice-cold champagne (see method)

Purée the mango and ginger in a blender with the ice. To serve, half-fill each glass with the mixture and top with champagne. Omit the ginger if preferred.

Serves 6 or more

Rosa-frizzare

A refreshing combination from Southern Italy. Mix ½ cup Campari and 2 cups grapefruit juice in a pitcher. To serve, half-fill each glass with the mixture, add ice, and top with champagne. For a special party, decorate with sprigs of mint.

Serves 6

Mandarin Fizz

Mix 4 cups mandarin juice and 1 cup Cointreau or Grand Marnier in a chilled pitcher. To serve, pour a little of the mixture into each glass, then top with champagne. For a single cocktail, omit the champagne and pour the fiery juice over ice.

Serves 12–16

Bellini Kir

Put about 2 tablespoons peach liqueur and a few slices of peach in each champagne glass and top with chilled champagne.

Serves 1 or many

The summery flavor of ripe red watermelon goes wonderfully well with the fresh, clean, lemony taste of gin. I grew up in the tropics, where there were lots of different watermelon varieties. The round ones with dark green skins and orange-red flesh were called sugar-melons, but the enormous torpedo-shaped ones with striped skins and pinky-red flesh were our favorites. The seed-free section in the middle of a melon is the sweetest, so if you're cutting pieces for a garnish, use this.

**2 very ripe watermelons,
well chilled
2–4 cups gin (or to taste)
to serve:
crushed ice
sprigs of mint
watermelon triangles (optional)**

watermelon
gin

Cut the watermelon in half and remove the rind and seeds. Purée the flesh in a blender or food processor. If the mixture is too thick, add water.

Pour into a pitcher, stir in the gin, and serve in small glasses with crushed ice, a sprig of mint, and a melon triangle.
Serves 4–6

Variation:
Lime and Watermelon Vodka
Substitute vodka instead of the gin, and stir in the juice of 2 limes.
Serves 4–6

negroni

One of the great classics—using Campari,
one of my favorite flavors—a little bitter,
a little sweet, a little smoky. It's a
stunning color—serve it in stemmed
glasses, over ice, "up with a twist"
as they say.

1 part Campari
1 part gin
1 part dry vermouth
ice
1 lemon slice or twist of lemon peel

Pour the first 3 ingredients into a glass, add
ice, stir, then decorate with a lemon slice or
a twist of lemon peel.
Serves 1

summer
cocktails

whiskey mac

Utterly delicious for people who like their drinks spicy but not too sweet. For a weaker version, serve in a tall glass and top up with a soft drink.

1 part whiskey
1 part green ginger wine
ice
a curl of lemon peel
gingerale or ginger beer (optional)

Shake the whiskey, ginger wine, and ice in a cocktail shaker. Strain into a small glass and serve with a curl of lemon peel.
Serves 1

Variation:
Whiskey Sour
Shake 1 jigger (about 3 tablespoons) bourbon or whiskey with the juice of half a lemon. Strain into a whiskey sour glass.
Serves 1

Traditionally, a mint julep should be served in a silver or pewter mug, so the frosty surface isn't marred by finger marks, but a chilled glass pitcher, frosty Collins glasses, and a drinking straw work just as well.

mint **julep**

24 mint leaves, torn, plus mint sprigs
3 tablespoons sugar syrup
1 teaspoon Angostura Bitters (optional)
1½ cups bourbon
ice cubes

Bruise the mint leaves in a tall glass, adding the sugar syrup and bitters, if using. Stir in the bourbon. Pack a chilled pitcher with ice and mint sprigs, then strain in the julep. Alternatively, pack tall glasses with ice, then pour in the julep. Serve with straws.
Serves 4

Variation:
Brandy Mint Julep
Substitute brandy instead of bourbon.
Serves 4

marvelous margarita

Margaritas are my favorite cocktail—great, and lethal when made properly—but sometimes almost totally without alcohol when ordered in a bar (probably a good idea!)

The usual way of serving margaritas is to rim the glasses with salt—this is optional, but I think that a twist of lime is absolutely crucial!

Some people also like a dash of sugar in this drink—though, in my opinion, this depends on the flavor of the limes.

Variations:

Frozen Margarita

In a blender, whizz 1 part tequila, 1 part Grand Marnier, 2 parts fresh lime juice, 2 parts ice, and sugar to taste, then pour into ice-frosted, salt-rimmed glasses.

Serves 1

Cranberry Margarita

In a blender, whizz 1 part each of tequila, Cointreau, and lime juice with 2 parts of cranberry juice, plus ice and sugar to taste.

Serves 1

1 part tequila

1 part triple sec or other orange liqueur, such as Cointreau

2 parts fresh lime juice, thinned with water if preferred

crushed ice or ice cubes

a twist of lime, to serve

Shake or blend the first 4 ingredients, then serve with a twist of lime.

Serves 1

morocco mary

The absolutely best Bloody Mary you ever tasted! I promise you! I have served this recipe to Bloody Mary purists and it was a huge success. In trying to emulate my efforts, one particularly purist friend added the harissa paste to his regular spicy recipe and wondered why some of his guests looked decidedly overheated!

1 teaspoon harissa paste

juice of 2 limes

¼ cup vodka

1 cup tomato juice

salt and freshly ground black pepper

ice

In a pitcher, mix the harissa, lime juice, and vodka, then the remaining ingredients. Alternatively, purée the harissa in a blender with the tomato juice and lime juice, then pour into the pitcher, stir in the vodka, and add salt and pepper to taste.

Serves 1–2

Variations:

Traditional Bloody Mary

Mix ¼ cup vodka with ½ cup tomato juice, the juice of 1 lemon, a dash each of Tabasco and Worcestershire sauce, and a pinch of celery salt. Stir well in a tall glass with ice cubes and serve with a celery stalk.

Virgin Mary

Omit the vodka and proceed as above.

Serves 1

Daiquiris always look so festive, and you can change the fruit to taste: pineapple or banana are both great! I like to use golden rum because it has a better taste —but the color will change somewhat.

frozen strawberry
daiquiri

juice of 2 limes

2 tablespoons sugar

½ cup white rum

6 strawberries

dash of strawberry liqueur (optional)

about 1 cup crushed ice

Purée all the ingredients in a blender until frothy, then pour into daiquiri glasses— preferably enormous!

Serves 2

Variations:

Lemon-Bacardi Daiquiri

In a blender, mix 3 parts Bacardi, 2 parts lemon juice, 1 part sugar syrup, and 1 cup ice.

Serves 4–5

Daiquiri Granita

Mix ⅓ cup each of sugar syrup and lime juice, 1½ cups rum, a dash of grenadine, and 1 cup ice in a blender. Serve in chilled glasses. (Sugar syrup is 2–3 parts water, 1 part sugar, boiled for 2 minutes, then cooled).

ginger rum

Rum and ginger are a marriage made in heaven—the very essence of the tropics! Golden rum from Barbados is a wonderful compromise between the elegance of white rum and the power-flavor of my favorite dark rum. The result is a delightful golden color. Serve as a cocktail, or as a long drink with your choice of mixer to make a drink more or less sweet.

1 piece stem ginger, crushed to a purée

1 teaspoon ginger syrup from the jar

¼ cup golden rum

1 tablespoon fresh lime juice

about ½ cup crushed ice or 6 ice cubes, plus extra, to serve

1 lime wedge

Crush the stem ginger to a purée with a fork, and scrape into a shaker. Add the ginger syrup, rum, lime juice, and ice. Shake well, then strain into a glass filled with ice and garnish with a wedge of lime. Add extra syrup if you prefer a sweeter drink. Alternatively, mix in a blender, then strain over ice.

For a long drink, serve in a Collins glass topped with ginger ale or soda.

Serves 1

a wonderful, golden cocktail with the
zippy spice of ginger

I grew up in tropical Australia, with wonderful, fresh, juicy, ripe pineapples and sweet dark Bundaberg rum—in our view the finest of all rums. However, it isn't a very pretty color when used with ingredients like these, so instead use a golden rum from Barbados or one of the other Caribbean islands. You could also use white rum, but it doesn't have the depth of flavor of the darker ones.

Australia also produces some of the world's finest ginger, which is exported all over the world. In this recipe, use preserved ginger in sugar syrup, or make your own fresh ginger purée by working peeled fresh ginger in a blender with a little lemon juice. You can spoon it into an ice cube tray, freeze it, and use a cube when you need it—in drinks, or cooking.

pineapple
rum

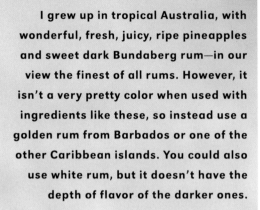

2 cups fresh pineapple juice
or 1 ripe pineapple, peeled and cored
2 tablespoons ginger purée or 2 pieces
preserved ginger, plus syrup, to taste
ice
1 cup white rum or golden rum
ginger beer or ginger ale (optional)

Blend the pineapple or juice with the puréed or preserved ginger and syrup. Strain into a pitcher of ice. Stir in the rum and serve immediately, or top with gingerale or ginger beer. Alternatively, strain into tall glasses full of ice, and top with gingerale.
Serves 4–6

Index

conversion chart

Weights and measures have been rounded up or down slightly to make measuring easier.

volume equivalents:

american	metric	imperial
1 teaspoon	5 ml	
1 tablespoon	15 ml	
¼ cup	60 ml	2 fl.oz.
⅓ cup	75 ml	2½ fl.oz.
½ cup	125 ml	4 fl.oz.
⅔ cup	150 ml	5 fl.oz. (¼ pint)
¾ cup	175 ml	6 fl.oz.
1 cup	250 ml	8 fl.oz.

weight equivalents:

imperial	metric
1 oz.	25 g
2 oz.	50 g
3 oz.	75 g
4 oz.	125 g
5 oz.	150 g
6 oz.	175 g
7 oz.	200 g
8 oz.	250 g
9 oz.	275 g
10 oz.	300 g
11 oz.	325 g
12 oz.	375 g
13 oz.	400 g
14 oz.	425 g
15 oz.	475 g
16 oz. (1 lb.)	500 g
2 1b.	1 kg

measurements:

inches	cm
¼ inch	5 mm
½ inch	1 cm
¾ inch	1.5 cm
1 inch	2.5 cm
2 inches	5 cm
3 inches	7 cm
4 inches	10 cm
5 inches	12 cm
6 inches	15 cm
7 inches	18 cm
8 inches	20 cm
9 inches	23 cm
10 inches	25 cm
11 inches	28 cm
12 inches	30 cm

oven temperatures:

225°F	110°C	Gas ¼
250°F	120°C	Gas ½
275°F	140°C	Gas 1
300°F	150°C	Gas 2
325°F	160°C	Gas 3
350°F	180°C	Gas 4
375°F	190°C	Gas 5
400°F	200°C	Gas 6
425°F	220°C	Gas 7
450°F	230°C	Gas 8
475°F	240°C	Gas 9

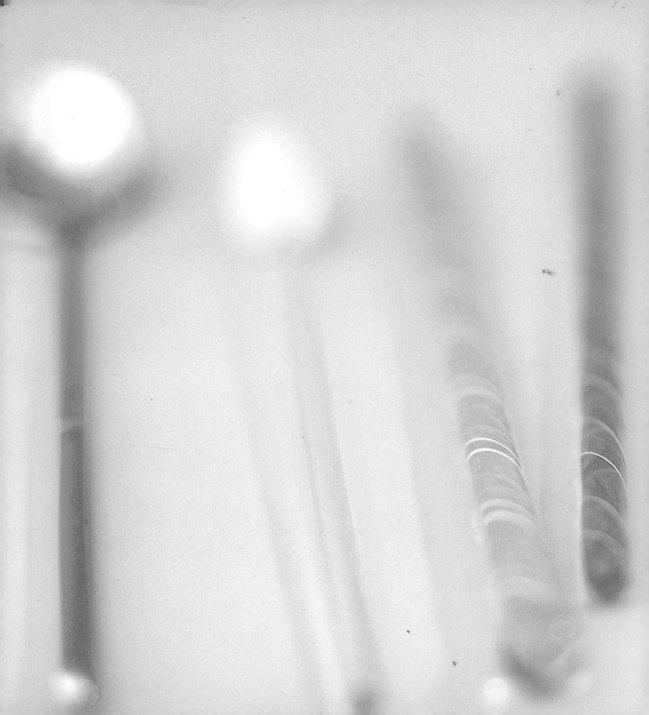